Taking a STANCE

a Guided Workbook for Teens

Learn the Power
of Aligning Your Body Language
with Your Words & Core Values

Taking a Stance: a Guided Workbook for Teens
Published by Taking a Stance Foundation, LLC

© 2020 Wayne Morris

All rights reserved. No portion of this book may be reproduced in any form without permission from the author, except as permitted by U.S. copyright law.

For permissions contact:
info@takingastancefoundation.com

ISBN: 978-0-578-68026-2

TABLE OF CONTENTS

Introduction: Your Core Values 1

The Disconnect 3

Achieving Alignment 5

Guard Against the World 7

Uniquely You 9

Maintaining Equilibrium 11

Your Winning Edge 13

INTRODUCTION: YOUR CORE VALUES

Values are your personal priorities, your beliefs, your driving forces. Identifying your values is key to creating powerful alignment between your body language and words.

Check the boxes that match your personal values. Feel free to add to the list:

- ☐ Acceptance
- ☐ Accountability
- ☐ Achievement
- ☐ Advancement
- ☐ Adventure
- ☐ Advocacy
- ☐ Ambition
- ☐ Appreciation
- ☐ Authenticity
- ☐ Balance
- ☐ Beauty
- ☐ Being the Best
- ☐ Benevolence
- ☐ Boldness
- ☐ Brilliance
- ☐ Calmness
- ☐ Caring
- ☐ Challenge
- ☐ Charity
- ☐ Cheerfulness
- ☐ Community
- ☐ Commitment
- ☐ Compassion
- ☐ Cooperation
- ☐ Collaboration
- ☐ Contribution
- ☐ Creativity
- ☐ Curiosity
- ☐ Daring
- ☐ Dedication
- ☐ Dependability
- ☐ Determination
- ☐ Development
- ☐ Empathy
- ☐ Encouragement
- ☐ Excellence
- ☐ Faith
- ☐ Fairness
- ☐ Family
- ☐ Friendships
- ☐ Flexibility
- ☐ Freedom
- ☐ Fun
- ☐ Generosity
- ☐ Grace
- ☐ Growth
- ☐ Happiness
- ☐ Health
- ☐ Honesty
- ☐ Humility
- ☐ Humor
- ☐ Independence
- ☐ Individuality
- ☐ Influence
- ☐ Innovation
- ☐ Inspiration
- ☐ Intelligence
- ☐ Joy
- ☐ Justice
- ☐ Kindness
- ☐ Leadership
- ☐ Learning
- ☐ Loyalty
- ☐ Making a Difference
- ☐ Mindfulness
- ☐ Motivation
- ☐ Optimism
- ☐ Originality
- ☐ Peace
- ☐ Professionalism
- ☐ Power
- ☐ Punctuality
- ☐ Quality
- ☐ Reliability
- ☐ Resilience
- ☐ Resourcefulness
- ☐ Responsibility
- ☐ Risk Taking
- ☐ Safety
- ☐ Security
- ☐ Self-Control
- ☐ Selflessness
- ☐ Service
- ☐ Simplicity
- ☐ Spirituality
- ☐ Stability
- ☐ Success
- ☐ Teamwork
- ☐ Thankfulness
- ☐ Uniqueness
- ☐ Versatility
- ☐ Wealth
- ☐ Well-Being
- ☐ Wisdom
- ☐ Zeal
- ☐ Other:

....
....
....
....
....
....
....
....

CHALLENGE YOUR THINKING:

Organize your values into 3 groups - grouping similar values together.

....
....
....
....
....
....

Select 1 value from each group that **best represents** that group.

1. ....
2. ....
3. ....

What do your personal values say about how you want to show up in the world? What is your **personal mission statement**? (What do you want to accomplish? Who do you want to help? What do you want to create?)

....
....
....
....
....
....
....

THE DISCONNECT

When there is a disconnect between your values, what you say with your words and what you "say" with your body language, it opens the door for misunderstanding.

Your body language is one factor in the perception others have of you and may influence how they treat you. While you cannot control what others think of you, you can control how you dress and how you carry yourself.

Let's explore the connection between how someone dresses and the perception of their values.

Gentlemen:	Ladies:
Have your intentions ever been misunderstood by someone else? If so, how were you dressed?	Have you ever been asked unwanted questions from a young man? If so, how were you dressed?
....	....
....	....
....	....
....	....
....	....
How does the way a young lady is dressed affect the way you approach her and your perception of her values?	How does the way a young man is dressed affect your perception of him and his values?
....	....
....	....
....	....
....	....
....	....

CHALLENGE YOUR THINKING:

Describe a time when you experienced **a disconnect** between your values and your words or your body language.

....
....
....

What reactions did you experience from others, and how did you feel?

....
....
....

What type of people do you attract when you have a disconnect between your values, words and body language?

....
....
....

Describe a time when you **misunderstood someone else** based on a disconnect in their values, words and body language.

....
....
....

How did you feel? How do you think they felt?

....
....
....

ACHIEVING ALIGNMENT

Alignment of your values with your dress and body language is achieved when a 'yes' or 'no' answer is understood just by looking at how you are dressed and how you carry yourself.

People use the way you dress and your body language as a way to "see" who you are and to "see" your values. If there is a question that you would say 'no' to, it should be known just by looking at you.

Let's examine what alignment "looks" like.

Gentlemen:	Ladies:
How should you dress to "show" that you would say 'no' to the following questions?	How should you dress to "show" that you would say 'no' to the following questions?
"Want to hang out and drink alcohol or do drugs?" "Let's go sell these drugs and make this money." "Want to go ___ (commit any crime)?"	"Want to hang out and drink alcohol or do drugs?" "Can I take you to a hotel or to my house?" "Can I give you a kiss?"
....	....
What do these questions tell you about how others perceive your values?	What do these questions tell you about how others perceive your values?
....	....

CHALLENGE YOUR THINKING:

What is the most common question that you have been asked where you had an **immediate** 'no' answer?

....
....
....

How were you dressed when asked that common question? Were you dressed in **alignment** with your values?

....
....
....

How can dressing and behaving **in alignment** with your values affect the reactions you get from others and their perception of your values?

....
....
....
....
....
....

What type of people do you **want** to attract with alignment in your values, words and body language?

....
....
....
....

GUARD AGAINST THE WORLD

Selfish indulgence, sex, promiscuity, drugs, and materialistic ambitions are tightly intertwined in our society. As we face these challenges, we need to observe the downside.

Let's compare and contrast values.

You:	Your Generation:
What are the 3 core values you identified previously?	What does your culture say that you should value most?
1.	1.
2.	2.
3.	3.
How does alignment, in your values, the way you dress and how you carry yourself, look?	How does your culture say you should dress and carry yourself?
Which of your goals and values are at risk if you follow the world's system?	What are the risks in indulging in the pleasures of the world without regard to your values?

Learn the Power of Aligning Your Body Language with Your Words & Core Values

CHALLENGE YOUR THINKING:

What bad influence caused you to change your **view on life** and your potential? How can you adjust your view to align with your values?

....
....
....
....
....
....

Do you own a lot of things or do they own you? How do you think about your material wealth? How important is it to you?

....
....
....
....
....
....

How will you **remind yourself** of your personal values and goals, and remind yourself of what is at risk by succumbing to the pleasures of the world?

....
....
....
....
....
....

UNIQUELY YOU

Just because there is a fashion trend, it doesn't mean you have to follow it. There is power in uniqueness. Don't be afraid to express your fashion in ways that align with your values.

The fashion, media and entertainment industries have a single mission — to influence your behavior.

Your power is in your ability to control your behavior, to create your own influence, and to choose fashion or start trends that reflect your personal values and mission statement.

Let's explore the fashion trends you follow, or create.

What fashion trends do you follow, or create? (Hair styles, clothes —revealing/tight/sagging— jewelry, tattoos)

....
....
....
....
....
....
....

When you dress to impress, how do you **want** others to perceive you?

....
....
....
....
....
....

CHALLENGE YOUR THINKING:

How is the fashion trend you follow, or create, **in alignment** with your values?

....
....
....
....
....

What **changes** can you make to the way you dress to create clear, consistent alignment with your values?

....
....
....
....
....
....
....
....
....
....
....
....
....
....
....

MAINTAINING EQUILIBRIUM

Maintaining alignment between values, words and behavior can be an internal struggle. Meditation is a powerful way to bring equilibrium to the mind and body.

Prayer is one form of meditation. If used right, meditation is like medicine to heal unresolved issues of your subconscious mind.

Your subconscious is constantly bombarded with images and ideas about who you are, what you should have, and what you should do. Influencers like media, marketing, social media, entertainment, society and culture all make an appeal to your subconscious. Why? It is your subconscious that impacts many of the important decisions you make.

Prayer, faith and spirituality have healing power to help you achieve inner alignment, heal your subconscious and improve behavior.

Let's explore the power of meditation.

What forms of meditation have you tried?

....

....

How has meditation positively impacted your well-being?

....

....

....

....

....

....

....

Brief Review

You have seen how a disconnect in your values, words and behavior can negatively impact how you are perceived and the reactions you receive from others. It also attracts the wrong people into your life - people who distract you from your goals.

Aligning your values, words and behavior has the power to attract the right people into your life - people who can help you achieve your goals and move forward on your journey.

Let's review what's at stake. Jot down a few of your goals and what you want to accomplish within the next 12 months.

....
....
....
....
....
....
....
....
....
....
....
....
....
....
....
....
....

YOUR WINNING EDGE

You possess within you, all the power you need to achieve alignment, maintain equilibrium, change your behavior and reach your goals.

Look at competitive athletes and others who have accomplished greatness in their field, such as: Mohammed Ali, Michael Jordan, Serena Williams, Jackie Robinson, Simone Biles, Denzel Washington, Viola Davis and Will Smith. What separates greatness achievers from greatness hopefuls is knowledge, determination and self-control.

Let's explore your winning edge.

Strengths:	Weaknesses:
What are your strengths?	In what areas can you improve?
....	....
....	....
....	....
What can you do to improve and further develop your strengths?	How can you use your strengths to minimize the impact of your weaknesses?
....	....
....	....
....	....
....	....
How can you use your strength to help someone else?	Who do you know that can help you improve your weaknesses?
....	....
....	....

Stand Strong

Negative desires and influences that come into your life are common to everyone. Many others have faced the exact same distraction as you are facing. Stand strong with knowledge, determination and self-control to persevere through the challenge. You will overcome and win!!

Take a few moments at the beginning or end of each day to meditate and visualize yourself overcoming any challenge you face. Journal the ideas and inspiration that comes to you through your mediation.

Let's review how YOU stand strong. Recall a time when you faced a negative influence and overcame it.

What strategies did you use?

....
....
....
....
....

How did it feel to be successful in overcoming?

....
....

How did the experience develop you?

....
....
....
....
....

Journal

Journal

Journal

Journal

Journal

Journal

Journal

Journal

YOU ARE NOT ALONE

The struggle is real...

As you strive to achieve and maintain internal well-being and alignment, you may need to reach out for help.

It's okay to ask for help!
Feel free to reach out to me, your teachers, counselors, mentor, youth leaders or any of the below organizations:

National Suicide Prevention Lifeline
1-800-273-8255

Crisis Text Line
Text HOME to 741741

Substance Abuse & Mental Health Services
Helpline: 1-800-622-4357

National Council on Alcoholism and Drug Dependence
HOPE Line: 1-800-622-2255

ABOUT THE AUTHOR

Growing up as the oldest male child in a single family home in North Carolina, Wayne Morris discovered early his natural ability to help others develop interpersonal skills and take an introspective look at how their thoughts, actions, and behaviors drive everything that happens around them, and ultimately their path in life.

Wayne has a solid foundation of faith, from which he has built successful businesses as an entrepreneur, including his Deep South Country Store Barbershop. Using his trade as a master barber, Wayne has taken his ministry of uplifting others into the county jail, where he helps these men rebuild themselves from the inside out. He augmented his skills and experience serving as a leader, coordinator, or case manager in various community organizations, such as: The Boys & Girls Club, a Police Community Center, local church youth groups, the Y.M.C.A, and Florida Healthy Start Organization.

At the culmination of 30+ years of experience, The Taking a Stance Foundation was birthed. Wayne designed a curriculum to teach at-risk youth ages 13-18 how to understand and embrace their value, and how to bring alignment to their values, words, dress and body language to unlock their inner power and ability to direct their path in life.

For more information on Wayne and the Taking a Stance Foundation, visit: www.takingastancefoundation.com

You are capable of greatness!

As you change your way of thinking,
it will lead to a change of heart -
a change of how you feel.
As you bring alignment to your life,
your behavior and decisions will change;
and you will find yourself a changed person
on the path to achieving more
than you ever dreamed possible!

Are you ready for the challenge?

www.ingramcontent.com/pod-product-compliance
Lightning Source LLC
Chambersburg PA
CBHW071419290426
44108CB00014B/1887